AN AMBIANCE/ALMOST FREE PLAYSCRIPT

DIRTY LINEN

and

NEW-FOUND-LAND

by TOM STOPPARD

Inter-Action Inprint, 14 Talacre Road, London NW5 3PE 1976

For Ed Berman

'Dirty Linen' was supposed to be a play to celebrate
Ed Berman's British naturalisation, but it went off
in a different direction — 'New-Found-Land' was
then written to re-introduce the American Connection.

For a fuller picture of certain allusions made in
'New-Found-Land', I refer the reader to Mr. Berman's
biographical note at the end of this volume.

T.S.

This playscript was first published to coincide with
the opening of 'Dirty Linen' and 'New-Found-Land'
at the Ambiance Lunch-Hour Theatre Club/Almost
Free Theatre

This second edition was published to coincide with
the transfer of the original production to the Arts
Theatre, London, where it re-opened on Wednesday,
16th June 1976.

Made and printed in England by Hill and Garwood Printing Ltd. , Wembley

CONTENTS

'DIRTY LINEN' and 'NEW-FOUND-LAND'
by **Tom Stoppard**

The first performances of 'Dirty Linen' and New-Found-Land' were at Inter-Action's Almost Free Theatre, Rupert Street, London W.1., on Tuesday 6th April 1976.
An Ambiance Lunch-Hour Theatre Club presentation with the following casts:

'DIRTY LINEN'

Maddie	Luan Peters
Cocklebury-Smythe, M.P.	Edward de Souza
McTeazle, M.P.	Benjamin Whitrow
Chamberlain, M.P.	Malcolm Ingram
Withenshaw, M.P. (the Chairman)	Peter Bowles
Mrs. Ebury, M.P.	Christine Ozanne
French, M.P.	Richard O'Callaghan
Home Secretary	Derek Ensor

'NEW-FOUND-LAND'

Arthur	Stephen Moore
Bernard	Richard Goolden

An Inter-Action production, designed by Gabriella Falk and directed by Ed Berman.

Production Manager and lighting	Suresa Galbraith
Administrator	Martin Turner
Stage Manager	Robin Hornibrook
Assistant Stage Manager	Brenda Lipson
Wardrobe Mistress	Carol Betera

Approximate playing time : 1 hour 25 minutes

DIRTY LINEN

a play in one act

CHARACTERS

MADDIE

COCKLEBURY-SMYTHE, M.P.

McTEAZLE, M.P.

CHAMBERLAIN, M.P.

WITHENSHAW, M.P.   (the CHAIRMAN)

Mrs. EBURY, M.P.

FRENCH, M.P.

HOME SECRETARY

*An overspill meeting room for House of Commons
business in the tower of Big Ben. A committee
table with chairs for everybody; separate table with
good slammable drawers for MADDIE; large blackboard on easel; shelves of files and books with
portable steps; and two doors.*

*The room is empty. MADDIE puts her head round
the door cautiously, enters in street coat and carrying
a small bag from a classy lingerie shop, and a handbag.
The room is unfamiliar to her. She hangs up her
coat on a coat/hat/umbrella stand which is just inside
the door, walks to the desk, and after a moment's
hesitation she takes a pair of silk, lace trimmed
French knickers out of the bag and puts them on.*

*MADDIE finishes putting on her knickers and drops
her skirt. The knickers ought to be remembered
for their colour — perhaps white silk with red lace
trimmings.*

*MADDIE is now wearing a low cut, sleeveless blouse,
buttoned insecurely down the front; a wrap-round
skirt, quite short; underneath, suspenders not tights,
and a waist-slip which is also pretty, silk and lace,
with a slit.*

*From her bag she takes a notebook and a pencil and
puts them on the desk. There are glasses and a
carafe on the large table. She picks up the lingerie
bag and looks around for a waste paper basket.
Finding none, she leaves by the other door, bag in
hand. The first door is now opened by McTEAZLE
who holds it open for COCKLEBURY-SMYTHE.*

C-S   *(entering)* Toujours la politesse.

McT   *(closing the door)* Noblesse oblige.

         *(They each carry several newspapers, a whole crop
         of the day's papers and the Sundays, which they
         dump on the big table. They doff their bowler
         hats and attempt to put them on the same peg.)*

McT   Mea culpa. *(courteously)*

C-S	Apres vous.
	(McTEAZLE *signals that* COCKLEBURY-SMYTHE *should hang up his hat first. They put their brollies in the umbrella stand.* COCKLEBURY-SMYTHE *sits down.)*
C-S	J'y suis, j'y reste.
	(He opens the Daily Mail.)
	Quel dommage.
McT	*(sitting down)* Le mot juste.
C-S	C'est la vie. Che sara sara. *(He throws the paper aside.)*
	(McTEAZLE *picks up the Daily Mirror and turns to page 3 which features a glamour picture, not particularly revealing.)*
McT	Ooh la-la! *(Then he recovers his dignity. Deprecatingly.)* Vox populi .... plus ca change, plus c'est la meme chose. *(He throws the paper aside and picks up the Guardian.)*
C-S	De gustibus non est disputandum.
	(Pause)
McT	*(hesitantly)* A propos .... entre nous .... vis-a-vis le Coq d'Or.
C-S	Ah, le Coq d'Or .....
McT	Faux pas, hein?
C-S	Ca ne fait rien.
McT	Bloody awkward though. Pardon my french.
	(MADDIE *re-enters with a waste-paperbasket.* McTEAZLE *does not see her as he is engrossed in The Guardian.* COCKLEBURY-SMYTHE *sees her but registers nothing.)*
C-S	Honi soit qui mal y pense. *(On which, without pausing he produces from an inside pocket a pair of french knickers and hands them to* MADDIE *as she crosses to her desk collecting them urbanely.)* Ergo nil desperandum.

McT   Absolutely!

> (COCKLEBURY-SMYTHE *picks up his copy of the* Daily Mirror *and turns to the pin-up on page 3. He makes a wordless noise appropriate to male approval of female pulchritude. This coincides with* MADDIE *bending over, showing cleavage, to put the knickers into a drawer of her desk. This moment of the man reacting to the pin-up photograph, and the coincidental image of* MADDIE *in a pin-up pose is something which is to be repeated several times, so for brevity's sake it will be hereafter symbolised by the expletive "Strewth!" It must be marked distinctly; a momentary freeze on stage, and probably a flash of light like a camera flash.* MADDIE *should look straight out at the audience for that moment.)*

C-S   Strewth!

> *(After the freeze* McTEAZLE *sees* MADDIE.*)*

McT   Good afternoon. *(He stands up.)* I am Mr. McTeazle and you are ...?

MADDIE   Miss Gotobed.

McT   Miss Gotobed. And this is Mr. Cocklebury-Smythe.

C-S   How do you do?

MADDIE   Hello.

C-S   So you are going to be our clerk.

MADDIE   Yes.

C-S   May I be the first to welcome you to Room 3b. You will find the working conditions primitive, the hours antisocial, the amenities non-existent and the catering beneath contempt. On top of that the people are for the most part very, very, very boring, with interests either so generalised as to mimic wholesale ignorance or so particular as to be lunatic obessions. Their level of conversation would pass without comment in the lavatory of a mixed comprehensive and the lavatories, by the way, are few and far between.

MADDIE   It has always been my ambition to work in the House of Commons.

(Sound of Big Ben chiming the half hour.)

C-S   Mine has always been the House of Lords.   But then perhaps I have not been willing to make the same sacrifices you have.

McT   Have you had to make sacrifices Miss Gotobed?   Not too arduous I hope?

MADDIE   It was hard work but I enjoyed the challenge.

C-S   *(quickly)*   Yes .... Yes, the P.M. offered me a life peerage, for services which he said he would let me know more about in due course if I were interested.   "I hear you're a keen gardener, Cockie" he said, "we can call it services to conservation".   "Not me, Rollo," I said, "All I use it for is a little topiary in the summer".   "Services to sport," he said — ignorant fool.   "No, no, Rollo" I said, "I really have no interests of any kind".   "That will be services to the arts", he said.   "Stop making such a fuss — do you want a life peerage or don't you?"   "No I don't" I said to him.   "What with only a couple of bachelor cousins in line ahead, one of whom is an amateur parachutist and the other a seamstress in the Merchant Navy I prefer to hang on for a chance of the real thing".   He said to me "My dear Cockie, life peers <u>are</u> the real thing nowadays".   "Oh no they're not, Rollo" I said. "That's just the kind of confusion you set up in people's minds by calling them Lord This and Lord That, pour encourager hoi polloi.   <u>They</u> think they're Lords — they skip off home and feed the budgerigar saying to themselves, My golly gorblimey, I'm a Lord!   They'd be just as happy if you suddenly told them they were all sheiks.   They'd put the Desert Song on the gramophone and clap their hands when they wanted their cocoa.   Now <u>you'd</u> know they're not really sheiks and <u>I'd</u> know they're not really sheiks, and God help them if they ever showed up east of Suez in their appalling pullovers with Sheik Shuttleworth stencilled on their airline bags — no my dear Rollo," I said, "I'll be a real peer or not at all".   "Now look here, Cockie," he said to me, "If they weren't real peers they wouldn't be in the House of Lords would they? — that's logic".   "If that's logic," I said "you can turn a regimental goat into a Lieutenant Colonel by electing it to the United Services Club".   "That's an interesting point,

Cockie," he said "It could explain a lot of my problems." Do you suppose we've got the wrong day? *(He takes out a pocket diary and consults it.)* Oh yes — Select Committee, House of Commons — take L.P. ...... take L.P. ......? What L.P?

MADDIE   It is the right day. I didn't get a wink of sleep all last night.

C-S   *(mutters)* L.P. ......

MADDIE   It's not every girl who gets advancement from the Home Office typing pool.

McT   I expect it's not every girl who proves herself as you have done, Miss Gotobed. Do you use Greggs or do you favour the Pitman method?

MADDIE   I'm on the pill.

(Small pause. McTEAZLE is expressionless.)

McT   Perhaps this might be an opportunity for me to explain to you the nature of the duties expected of a secretary/clerk attached to a Select Committee, duties which for one reason or another you may have got confused in your mind.

C-S   *(suddenly)* Lace panties. Sorry.

McT   Now, this is a meeting of a Select Committee of Members of Parliament to report on moral standards in the House — not in the House literally, or rather, in the House literally but also, and for the most part, outside the House too.

MADDIE   In the car park?

McT   Not literally in the car park — or rather in the car part too, yes, but also — don't try to take in more than you can. Now, this is a continuation of a Select Committee set up during the last session of Parliament, though at that time the member-ship of the Committee was different. A Select Committee must be reconvened with each new session of Parliament, and it is this reconstituted Committee which is about to begin sitting to report on rumours of sexual promiscuity by certain unspecified Members which, if substantiated, might tend to bring into disrepute the House of Commons and possibly the

Lords and one or two government departments including Social Security, Environment, Defence, Health, Agriculture and even, I'm sorry to say, the Milk Marketing Board.

MADDIE   Why's that?

McT   Because I have the honour to be on that Board and I think I can say without fear of contradiction that the MMB has an unrivalled record of freedom from suggestions of being a sexual free-for-all, and furthermore we are now getting yoghurt and single and double cream to every corner of —

MADDIE   Actually what I meant was, why would it bring them into disrepute?

McT   Because the country by and large looks to its elected representatives to set a moral standard.

MADDIE   No it doesn't —

McT   *(smoothly)* No it doesn't — you're quite right. Then it's because the authority of the — er — authorities is undermined by losing the respect of —

MADDIE   I don't think people care.

McT   No, people don't care — of course they don't. In which case I think it is fair to say that this Committee owes its existence to the determination of the Prime Minister to keep his House in order, whatever the cost in public ridicule, whatever the consequence to people in high places, and to the fact that the newspapers got wind of what was going on. It is unfortunate that the well known restraint and sense of higher purpose which characterises the British press — a restraint which would have treated with utter contempt stories of garter-snapping by a few M.P.s — gave way completely at the rumour that they were all snapping the same garter. You may know, if you are a student of the press, or if you have at any time in the last few weeks passed within six feet of a newspaper, that there is no phrase as certain to make a British sub-editor lose his sense of proportion as the phrase "Mystery Woman". This Committee was set up at the time when the good name of no fewer than 21 Members of Parliament was said to have been compromised. Since then rumour has fed on rumour and we face the possibility that a sexual swathe has passed through Westminster claiming the reputations of, to put no finer point upon it, 119 Members.   Someone is going through the ranks like a lawnmower in knickers.   Well, I need hardly say *(He is taking papers out of his brief case.)* that we as a Committee are working in a sensitive area, one which demands great tact on all our parts —

> (McTEAZLE *produces from his brief case a pair of knickers and hands them to* MADDIE.)

your own not excluded.

> (MADDIE *collects the knickers urbanely and puts them in her knicker drawer; she has changed her position however and has to practically sprawl across the desk to do this, thus showing leg as well as cleavage.   Simultaneously* COCKLEBURY-SMYTHE *has discovered a pin-up picture in the Daily Mail, or any other appropriate paper except the Sun.)*

C-S   Strewth!

> *(After the freeze there seems to be nothing to occupy the two men.   MADDIE collects herself and sits demurely on her desk.   The two men try to get close to* MADDIE *without the other noticing.)*

C-S   Well, this is getting us nowhere.   Where is everybody?

> *(In the following section, the underlined words are said privately to* MADDIE *with no change of tone or volume while the other is at the extreme of his perambulation.)*

C-S   Are we going to have a quorum?   You may not be familiar with the term quorum incidentally <u>if anyone asks you where you had dinner last night</u> it's a Latin word meaning of 'which or of whom ......

McT   Quite simply, it's the smallest number of members of a committee necessary to constitute the said committee, for example, say you were <u>nowhere near the Coq d'Or on Satur-day night</u> then the smallest number of members without which a quorum can't be said to be a quorum —

C-S   A quorum is nothing more or less than the largest minimum specified number of members being that proportion of the

whole committee, let us say three or four-<u>get Coq d'Or</u>
<u>Sunday night completely</u> invalid without them.   Got it?

McT   It's not as complicated as it sounds.

MADDIE   Is it a specified number of members of a committee whose
                   presence — God bless them — is necessary for the valid
                   transaction of business by that committee?

McT   Yes .... Yes, that is pretty well what a quorum is.   I can see,
                   Miss Gotobed, that there is more to you than your name
                   might suggest — by which I mean *(trying to accelerate out*
                   of trouble) that you don't spend all your time flat on your
                   back — or your front — your side, flat on your side, sleeping,
                   fast asleep, when you could be doing your homework
                   instead of living up to your name, which you don't, that's
                   my point.

                           (COCKLEBURY-SMYTHE has been standing like
                           stone, his glazed eyes absently fixed on MADDIE's
                           cleavage.)

C-S   McTeazle, why don't you go and see if you can raise those
                   great tits — boobs — those boobies, absolute tits, don't you
                   agree, Malcolm and Douglas — though good men as well, of
                   course, useful chaps, very decent, first rate, two of the best,
                   Malcolm and Douglas, why don't you have a quick poke, peek,
                   in the Members Bra — or the cafeteria, they're probably
                   guzzling coffee (MADDIE *crosses her legs)* and Swedish panties -
                   Danish, I'll tell you what, why don't you go and see if you can
                   raise Malcolm and Douglas — *(to* MADDIE) sometimes there
                   are more of these committees trying to meet than there are
                   rooms for them to meet in — that's why we're up here in the
                   tower instead of one of those nice rooms on the Committee
                   Floor with the green leather chairs, though I expect you've
                   spent a lot of time on the Floor, Miss Gotobed, by which I
                   mean, of course, the Committee Bed, Floor -- *(getting hyster-*
                   ical) McTeazle the Division Bell will go before we even get
                   started and then we'll all have to go off and vote on some
                   beastly amendment to make anyone who buys his own council
                   house a life bishop with the right to wear a nightie on his head
                   — mitre on his head.   My God, I could do with a drink —

McT   You go then.   No, I'll go.   I'll tell you what, Miss Gotobed,
                   why don't you come with me, I'll show you round the lavatories

round the House, show you the Chamber, the lavatories —

C-S   She doesn't want to go trudging round the House inspecting the toilets like a deputation from the Water Board. Let the poor girl alone — she didn't get a wink of sleep all night.

>*(He ushers McTEAZLE out and closes the door. He turns and addresses MADDIE immediately. In the following speech the underlined words coincide with McTEAZLE's brief re-appearance to take his bowler hat off the hatstand.)*

C-S   Maddie my dear, you look even more ravishing this afternoon than <u>the smallest specified number of members of that committee of which</u> we will have to be very, very careful — it is a cruel irony that our carefree little friendship, which is as innocent and pure as the first driven snowdrop of spring, is in danger of being trampled by the hobnailed hue-and-cry over these absurd rumours of unbuttoned behaviour in and out of both trousers of parliament — I think I can say, and say with confidence, that when the smoke has cleared from the Augean stables, the little flame of our love will still be something no-one else can hold a candle to so long as we can keep our heads down. In other words, my darling girl, if anyone were to ask you where you had lunch on Friday, breakfast on Saturday or dinner on Sunday, best thing is to forget Crockfords, Claridges and the Coq d'Or.

MADDIE   *(concentrating)* Crockfords — Claridges — the Coq d'Or.

C-S   Forget — forget.

MADDIE   Forget. Forget Crockfords, Claridges, Coq d'Or. Forget Crockfords, Claridges, Coq d'Or. *(to herself)* Forget Crockfords, Claridges, Coq d'Or. Forget Crockfords, Claridges, Coq d'Or.

>*(COCKLEBURY-SMYTHE sees that this is achieving the opposite.)*

C-S   Alright — tell you what — say you had <u>breakfast</u> at Claridges, <u>lunch</u> at the Coq d'Or, and had <u>dinner</u> at Crockfords. Meanwhile I'll stick to —

MADDIE   *(concentrating harder than ever)* Claridges, Coq d'Or, Crockfords. Forget Crockfords, Claridges, Coq d'Or. Remember

Claridges, Coq d'Or, Crockfords.   Remember Claridges,
Coq d'Or, Crockfords.   Claridges, Coq d'Or, Crockfords,
Claridges, Coq d'Or, Crockfords.

C-S   But not with me.

MADDIE   Not with you.   Not with Cockie at Claridges, Coq d'Or,
             Crockfords.   Never at Claridges, Coq d'Or, Crockfords
             with Cockie.   Claridges, Coq d'Or, Crockfords.   Claridges,
             Coq d'Or, Crockfords.

> *(Her concentration doesn't imply slowness: she
> is fast, eager, breathless, very good at tongue
> twisters.   Her whole attitude in the play is one
> of innocent, eager willingness to please.
> COCKLEBURY-SMYTHE sees that he is going
> about this the wrong way.)*

C-S   Wait a minute.   *(rapidly)*   The best thing is, forget Claridges,
             Crockfords and the Coq d'Or altogether.

MADDIE   Right!   Forget Claridges, Crockfords, Coq d'Or —
             Forget Claridges, Crockfords, Coq d'Or —

C-S   And if anyone asks you where you had lunch on Friday,
             breakfast on Saturday and dinner last night, when you were
             with me, tell them where you had dinner on Friday, lunch
             on Saturday and breakfast yesterday.

MADDIE   Right!

> *(Pause.   MADDIE closes her eyes with concentration.)*

             (rapidly)   The Green Cockatoo, the Crooked Clock, the Crock
             of Gold — and Box Hill.

C-S   Box Hill?

MADDIE   To see the moon come up — forget Crockfords, Claridges,
             Coq d'Or — remember the Crock of Gold, Box Hill, the
             Crooked Clock and the Green Door —

C-S   Cockatoo —

MADDIE   Cockatoo.   Crock of Gold, Crooked Clock, Green Cockatoo
             and Box Hill.   When was this?

C-S   When you were really with me.

MADDIE   Right. With Cockie at the Green Cockatoo —

C-S   No, not with Cockie at the Green Cockatoo.

MADDIE   — not with Cockie at the Green Cockatoo, the Old Cook, the Crooked Grin, Gamages and Box Hill.

C-S   *(wildly)* No — look. The simplest thing is to forget, Claridges, the Old Boot, the Golden quorum can be any number agreed upon by —

            (This is because McTEAZLE is back)

McT   Douglas is on his way. *(Hanging up his hat.)*

C-S   I've got to have a drink.

            (He leaves, forgetting his bowler hat, as McTEAZLE closes the door. McTEAZLE starts speaking at once. The underlined words correspond to COCKLEBURY-SMYTHE's momentary reappearances, in the first case to take a bowler hat off the hatstand and in the second case to change hats because he has taken out McTEAZLE's hat the first time.)

McT   Maddie—ning the way one is kept waiting for ours is a very tricky position, my dear.   In normal times one can count on chaps being quite sympathetic to the sight of a Member of Parliament having dinner with a lovely young woman in some out of the way nook — it could be a case of constituency business, they're not necessarily screw—oo—oge is, I think you'll find, not in David Copperfield at all, still less in The Old Curiosity Sho—cking though it is, the sight of a Member of Parliament having some out-of-the-way nookie with a lovely young woman might well be a case of a genuine love match destined to take root and pass through ever more respectable stages — the first shy tentative dinner party in a basement flat in Pembridge Crescent for a few trusted friends — Caxton Hall — and a real friendship with stepchildren — people are normally inclined to give one the benefit of the doubt.   But the tragedy is, as our luck would have it, that our gemlike love which burns so true and pure and has brought such a golden light into our lives, could well become confused with a network of grubby affairs between men who should know better and some bit of fluff from the filing department — so I suggest, my darling, if any one were to enquire where you may or may not have spent Friday night or indeed Saturday lunch time or Sunday tea time, forget Charing Cross, the Coq d'Or and the Golden Ox.

MADDIE   Charing Cross, Coq d'or, Golden Ox.   Charing Cross, Coq d' Or, Golden Ox.   Charing Cross, Old Door, and the Golden Cock —

McT   — Ox —

MADDIE   Ox.

McT   The Coq d'Or and the Golden Ox.   Not the Golden Cock and the Old Door.

MADDIE   Not the Golden Cock and the Old Door but the Golden Ox and the Coq d'Or.

McT   And don't forget: Charing Cross.

MADDIE   Don't forget Charing Cross.

McT   I mean forget Charing Cross.

MADDIE   Forget Charing Cross —

McT   Plucky girl —

MADDIE   Plucky girl — Charing Cross — Olden Cocks.

McT   But not with me.

MADDIE   Not with Jock at the Old Cock —

McT   Door   *(This is because the door has opened.)*

MADDIE   Old Coq d'Or — not with Jock.
                    (CHAMBERLAIN *has entered.)*

McT   *(hurriedly)*   Hello, Douglas.

(CHAMBERLAIN *is repellently full of zest and*
heartiness. He also carries an armful of papers
which he dumps on the bable. He treats MADDIE
with open, crude, lechery.)

CHAMB Hello!

McT This is Mr. Chamberlain. Miss Gotobed is going to be our
clerk.

(CHAMBERLAIN *advances on* MADDIE *who backs*
off behind her desk and starts opening drawers to
look busy.)

CHAMB What?! — that luscious creature is our clerk! Impossible!
Where's her moustache? Her dandruff? Her striped pants?
(MADDIE *reflexively slams shut her knicker drawer.)* What
an uncommonly comely clerk you are! My name's Douglas.
I hope you don't mind me saying that you're a lovely girl —
I don't mind telling you that if I wasn't married to a wonderful girl myself with two fine youngsters down in Dorking and
an au pair to complicate my life, I'd be after you and no
mistake,

(*During the rest of this speech,* MADDIE *pushes past*
CHAMBERLAIN, *goes over to her coat and takes a*
copy of the Sun from her pocket. She returns
towards her desk.)

my goodness, yes, it would be private coaching in a little
French restaurant somewhere, a few hints on parliamentary
procedure over the boeuf bourgignon, and then off in the
Volvo while I mutter sweet definitions in your ear and test
your elastic with the moon coming up over Box Hill.

(*As* MADDIE *passes the steps, he gooses her so*
thoroughly that she goes straight up them, still
holding the Sun. CHAMBERLAIN *slaps a sheet*
of paper on her desk.)

Have you an order of business? *(He turns aside.)*
Well, well, here we are without a quorum and I thought I was
going to be late. *(to* MADDIE) You'll know, of course, that
a quorum is a specified number of members of a committee
whose presence — God bless them— is necessary for the valid
transaction of business by that committee — got it? Good.

(CHAMBERLAIN *opens the Daily Mirror to the pin-up*

page. McTEAZLE *helps* MADDIE *down the steps;*
her skirt comes away in his hand.)

Strewth!

(After the freeze McTEAZLE *tries to shove the skirt*
at MADDIE *who has sat down primly behind her desk,*
but COCKLEBURY-SMYTHE *enters so* McTEAZLE
sits on the skirt.)

C-S   Do we have a quorum?

CHAMB   Hello, Cocklebury-Smythe.

C-S   So glad you could come, Chamberlain. You know Miss Gotobed

CHAMB   *(over-reacts)* No.

C-S   Mr. Chamberlain — Miss Gotobed.

CHAMB   I meant I didn't <u>know</u> her.

C-S   Of course you don't know her.   All we need now is our Chair-
           man.   I wish he'd get his clogs on.

           (The door opens and WITHENSHAW, *the Chairman,*
           enters.   He is a Lancastrian.   He also carries news-
           papers and a brief case.)

WITHEN   There's trouble in t'Mail.

C-S   Mill.

WITHEN   Mail. *(He throws the papers and his brief case onto the table.)*

C-S   Oh yes.

WITHEN   *(at* MADDIE)   And who have we got here?

MADDIE   I'm the clerk.   Miss Gotobed.

WITHEN   And I'm Malcolm Withyou!   *(He laughs uproariously.)*
           Malcolm Withyou! — 'ee you've got to be quick — Malcolm
           Withenshaw, Chairman of Select Committee on Promiscuity
           in High Places.   Have you got an order of business?   *(He*
           snatches CHAMBERLAIN's *piece of paper off her desk.)*

22

"Forget Golden Goose, Selfridges — "

> (MADDIE *snatches the paper out of his hand and hands him in the same movement a sealed envelope from her bag.*)

MADDIE   This is for you.

WITHEN   *(generally)* Before I saw bloody paper I was going to congratulate you all on a clean bill of health. You can't have a committee washing dirty linen in the corridors of power unless every member is above suspicion.

> (*On which he produces from the envelope a large pair of Y-front pants which he immediately shoves back into the envelope.*)

The wheres and Y-fronts, the whys and wherefores of this Committee are clear to you all. Our presence here today is testimony to the trust the House has in us as individuals and that includes you Maddiemoiselle. *(to MADDIE)* Though you have been completely unaware of it your private life has been under intense scrutiny by top man in Security Service, a man so senior that I can't even tell you his name —

MADDIE   Fanshawe.

WITHEN   Fanshawe — and you passed test.

> (*He has been looking around for a place to put his pants, and decides on MADDIE's desk drawer.*)

Indeed the fact that you've jumped over heads of many senior clerks indicates that you passed with flying knickers.

> (*This slip of the tongue is because he has discovered the knickers in the drawer; he drops them back and slams the drawer.*)

So it is all the more unfortunate to find stuff in the press like following :- Thank you, Cockie.

> (COCKLEBURY-SMYTHE *reads from the Daily Mail.*)

C-S   "On the day the Select Committee on Moral Standards in Public Life is due to reconvene I ask — was it wise for one of the members to be seen holding hands under the table with a staggeringly voluptuous, titian-haired, green eyed beauty in a West End restaurant at the weekend?   And if so, was it modest to chose the Coq d'Or?"

> *(Meanwhile, WITHENSHAW has finished scribbling a note.)*

WITHEN Right.   Bloody smart alec.   Still, least said soonest mended.

> *(He tosses the note, which is on white paper the size of an old-fashioned £5 note, onto MADDIE's desk.)*

Now then, I think you have received prior copies of my draft report, and we'll go through it paragraph by paragraph in the usual way —

McT Excuse me.   Are we now in session?

WITHEN What's quorum Miss Gotobed?

MADDIE Is it a specified number of —

CHAMB *(hurriedly)*   Four, Mr. Chairman.

WITHEN Then we'll kick off.   Get your pencil out, lass.

MADDIE Do I have to write down what you say?

WITHEN I can see you know your way around these committees, Miss Gotobed.   You do speedwriting I suppose?

MADDIE Yes, if I'm given enough time.

WITHEN That's alright.   You just tell us if we're going too fast. Here's a copy of my draft report, and appendix A, B, C, and D,

> *(He is giving her these things out of his brief case, into which he puts the envelope containing his pants.)*

so it'll just be a matter of keeping a record of amendments, if any.

C-S Excuse me, Withenshaw, but isn't it rather unusual to have a report by a Select Committee before the Committee has had the advantage of considering the evidence?

WITHEN   Yes, it is unusual, Mr. Cocklebury-Smythe, but this is an unusual situation.   As you know sexual immorality unites all parties.   This Committee isn't here to play politics. You'll have your chance with amendments, for which you can have all the time in the world.   In fact the P.M. insists on it — he doesn't want us to rush into print, he wants a thorough job which he can present to the House the day before the Queen's Silver Jubilee, along with trade figures.

McT   Isn't that going to cause rather a lot of flak in the 1922 Committee and the P.L.P?

WITHEN   Very likely, but by that time, I'm happy to say, I'm going to be well out of it in Lords — Life Peerage for services to arts.

C-S   Services to the <u>arts?</u>

WITHEN   I'll have you bloody know Mrs. Withenshaw and I have personally donated the Boticelli-style painted ceiling in the Free Church Assembly Hall.   I've bought and paid for more naked bums than you've had hot dinners.

C-S   I'm glad to say I've had more hot dinners.

WITHEN   I speak sub-cathedra of course — no one else knows except Mrs. Withenshaw, and I shouldn't have told her — she's taken to wearing white gloves up to elbows to greyhounds. Anyway, what the P.M. wants is a unanimous report, if possible declaring *(as if remembering)* that there is no evidence that Members have engaged in scandalous conduct above national average, or alternatively that they may have done in isolated cases, but are we going to judge grown responsible men in this day and age by the standards of Mrs. Grundy — whoever she may be — is it that old bag from Chorleywood South?

C-S   But what's the report based on if we aren't going to call any witnesses?

WITHEN   What witnesses do you want to call?

C-S   Well .... I personally wouldn't wish to call any —

McT	Hear, hear!
CHAMB	Absolutely!
C-S	I've no time for stool pigeons admittedly —
McT	Hear, hear!
CHAMB	Absolutely!
WITHEN	There aren't any bloody witnesses. No-one has seen anything. It's all bloody innuendo to sell newspapers in slack period.
ALL	Hear, hear!
WITHEN	What with giant killers knocked out of Cup, and Ceylon versus Bangladesh — I don't call <u>that</u> a bloody test match — the papers naturally resort to sticking their noses into upper reaches of top drawers looking for hankie panties, etcetera ....
ALL	Hear, hear!
WITHEN	I tell you, if those bloody pandas had got stuck in and produced a cuddly black and white nipper for London Zoo, it wouldn't be <u>us</u> in spotlight —
ALL	Hear, hear!
WITHEN	Or Mark and Anne for that matter.
C-S	Steady on, Malcolm.
WITHEN	I don't mean it would be black and white.
C-S	Can we move on — ?
WITHEN	I was just making the point that there's nothing to witness, just because a member of this Committee is so bowed down with the burden of representing his constituency, while trying to make a decent living in his spare time, that he has to take his — homework — to lunch in a West End restaurant.
ALL	Hear, hear!

CHAMB	Or to dinner — pilloried for a beef stew in a modest eating house with a professional appointment, for all anyone knows a vicar's daughter worried sick about the new motorway.
McT	Any cynic can make it look like a hole-in-the-corner affair in an out-of-the-way nook like the Coq d'Or — quite probably is, many of these French places are —
C-S	Nor was it a case of holding hands under the table.
ALL	Hear, hear!
C-S	Probably she was passing him the money under the table, or vice versa.
McT	The table under the money —
C-S	— him passing her the money under the table — probably a financially embarrassed lobbyist for sexual equality taking an M.P. to a working dinner.
McT	Women's lib —
WITHEN	One of those American bits.
C-S	Quite possibly —
WITHEN	These Americans, they get in everywhere.
C-S	Far·too many of them about.
McT	Hear, hear!
CHAMB	Absolutely!
WITHEN	*(to* MADDIE) Would you care to take my appendix out and pass it around — I've got something of a reputation for dry humour, you know. Yes, I once took a train journey right across America ....

> *(He pauses at the sight of* MADDIE *in her slip.*
> MADDIE *has picked up the sets of appendices*
> *and come out from behind her desk and taken*

*(two steps before remembering her state of undress,
she pauses at the same moment, and then decides
to continue. Big Ben starts chiming the three-
quarter hour. MADDIE goes round the table
placing documents in front of the first couple of
places. Big Ben finishes chiming the three-quarter
hour.)*

.... but that's another story.

*(The door opens to admit Mrs. EBURY. All look
at her as she speaks except McTEAZLE, who tries
to hand MADDIE her skirt unnoticed. MADDIE
misses this, as she is intent on passing out the rest
of the appendices.)*

Mrs. E   I'm sorry to be late Malcolm.

WITHEN   Come right in Deborah — we're just casting our eye over the
media. You're next to me, lass.

*(Mrs. EBURY hangs up her coat. She also is carrying
newspapers and brief case. To get round the table
she has to pass behind the blackboard, as does
MADDIE who is making slightly heavy weather of
sorting out appendices A, B, C, and D for each
member. Mrs. EBURY and MADDIE cross over
behind the blackboard but do not emerge immed-
iately. Meanwhile the CHAIRMAN has opened the
leader page of the Times and has started reading
aloud.)*

WITHEN   "Cherchez La Femme Fatale. It needs no Gibbon come
from the grave to spell out the danger to good government
of a moral vacuum at the centre of power. Even so, Rome
did not fall in a day, and mutatis mutandis it is not yet a
case of sauve qui peut for the government — " — what is all
this? — "Admittedly the silence hangs heavy in the House,
no doubt on the principle of qui s'excuse s'accuse, but we
expect the electorate to take in its stride cum grano salis
stories that upwards of a hundred M.P.s are in flagrante
delicto, still more that the demi-mondaine in most cases is
a single and presumably exhausted du Barry de nos jours
— " bloody 'ell. *(to McTEAZLE)* What does yours say?

McT   *(reading from The Guardian)* "Specialités de la Maison."

MADDIE   *(only her legs visible behind the blackboard)* Forget the
            Golden Carriage, the Cooking Pot and the Coq d'Or.
            Forget the Golden Carriage, the Watched Pot and the Coq
            d'Or.   Forget the Golden Pot, Claridges and the Watched
            Cook ....

            (MADDIE's *speech is soft until* McTEAZLE
            reaches "tedious, or at any rate tendentious
            ..." *where it stops, to be heard again on*
            McTEAZLE's "Quis custodiet ...." *and finally
            stopping on* WITHENSHAW's "Information".)

McT   The House of Commons is no stranger to scandal or to
            farce but it usually manages to arrange its follies so as to
            keep the two separate.   It would be tedious, or at any rate
            tendentious, to give a catalogue raisonée of the, at a
            Conservative estimate 63 Members of Parliament, and at
            a Labour estimate 114, of whom the homme moyen sensuel
            on the Clapham omnibus might well be asking, "Quis
            custodiet ipsos custodes?"

            (Mrs. EBURY *emerges during this final Latin
            phrase.   Her hair, which had been done up in
            a bun, is now about her shoulders and her
            buttoned-up suit is in discreet disarray.   She
            takes her seat.)*

            (continuing) "– and yet our information –"

            (MADDIE *emerges from behind the blackboard.)*

WITHEN   *(scornfully)* Information!   What does the Editor of
            Manchester Guardian know about anything – bloody
            young pup – what's his name –

MADDIE   *(putting documents in front of him)* Peter.

WITHEN   *(to* Mrs. EBURY) Ah – I don't think you know
            Miss Gotobed.

Mrs. E   How do you do?

MADDIE   Hello!

            (CHAMBERLAIN *picks up the Daily Mirror.)*

CHAMB   "How many cocks on the dung heap?   We say too

see page 2." *(He turns the page and shows WITHENSHAW.)*

> *(McTEAZLE is surreptitiously trying to shove MADDIE's skirt at her as she goes by. She doesn't notice, and he grabs at her slip.)*

WITHEN   Strewth!

> *(ALL but McTEAZLE look at him — ALL freeze. Simultaneously MADDIE's slip has come away in McTEAZLE's hand, leaving her wearing a revealing blouse, knickers, suspender belt, stockings and shoes.*
>
> *After the freeze MADDIE sits down behind her desk. The CHAIRMAN hastily folds up the Mirror and puts it aside. McTEAZLE now sits on the skirt and the slip.)*

WITHEN   *(to MADDIE)* Well, are you ready for it Miss Gotobed?

MADDIE   Yes.

WITHEN   Well we seem to be a full complement except for Mr. French. Has anybody heard whether he's coming?

Mrs. E   I hope to God not.

WITHEN   Mr. French always has the best interests of the House at heart. That's why he comes over as a sanctimonious busybody with an Energen roll where his balls ought to be — no need to start writing yet, Miss Gotobed.

McT   I don't know what the P.M. was thinking of.

C-S   I expect he was thinking of having a balanced committee to lend the kind of credibility to our report which has eluded him in public life.

WITHEN   *(to MADDIE)* Not yet. *(stands)* Now, as this Select Committee has, as it were, lost its Chairman of the last session, our first duty as a Committee is to make good that loss.

> *(Very rapidly now.)*

Propose Mr. Withenshaw.

McT	Second.
WITHEN	Any other nominations? The question is put —
ALL	Aye.
WITHEN	Thank you Mrs. Ebury and gentlemen. *(sits)* Let's get started. *(to* MADDIE*)* Mr. Withenshaw called to chair. The Chairman's draft report, having been read for the first time — any objections? — thank you — was further considered as follows :-
	Paragraph 1. In performing the duty entrusted to them your Committee took as their guiding principle that it is the just and proper expectation of the electorate and the country at large, that its representatives in parliament should bring probity, honourable intent and decent conduct not merely to the discharge of the business of government but also to their personal and social behaviour, which needs must stand in an exemplary relationship to the behaviour of the British people generally.
C-S	I must say that strikes an authentic Lancastrian note. Who wrote this?
WITHEN	Would you mind?
C-S	Was it the P.M?
WITHEN	No.
C-S	I'll know if it becomes Tennysonian, you know.
WITHEN	You're out of order Mr. Cocklebury-Smythe.
	(MADDIE *has her hand up, the other hand writing busily but laboriously.)*
WITHEN	Not that bit, Miss Gotobed.
MADDIE	"…. called to chair."
C-S	The chair.

WITHEN	*(at MADDIE's speed which is about 30 words a minute)* "The chair. The Chair-man's draft report having been read for the first time was further con-sider-ed as fol-lows —" The next bit is the draft report, and you've already got that so you don't have to write it down again.
MADDIE	*(with the document)* All this about setting an example?
WITHEN	Yes.
MADDIE	You should tell them to mind their own business.
WITHEN	Who?
MADDIE	Whoever it is who wants to know. It's a load of rubbish.
WITHEN	What is?
MADDIE	People don't care what M.P.s do in their spare time, they just want them to do their jobs properly bringing down prices and everything.
WITHEN	Yes, well ....
MADDIE	Why don't they have a Select Committee to report on what M.P.s have been up to in their working hours — that's what people want to know.
C-S	It's rather more complicated than that — er — Arab oil and ....
	(The following speeches overlap each other until the CHAIRMAN calls the meeting to order.)
CHAMB	..... the Unions.
C-S	M.P.s don't have the power they used to have, you know.
McT	Foreign exchange — the Bank of England.
Mrs. E	The multi-national companies.
McT	Not to mention government by Cabinet.
CHAMB	Government by Cabal.

Mrs. E	Brussels.
C-S	The Whips.
WITHEN	Just a minute — that'll do — come to order.
MADDIE	I'm sorry.
WITHEN	Paragraph 2. Your Committee took it as self-evident that the consent to govern may be withheld if the people lose respect for the Commons either severally or as an institution, either through executive or constitutional deficiency, either on practical or moral grounds. It is on this latter ground — the morality of the honourable 600 — that your Committee has fixed its lance, determined to ride fearlessly into the jaws of controversy.
C-S	It is the P.M., isn't it?
WITHEN	I'm not saying it is, and anyway what's wrong with Her Majesty's first minister keeping a watchful eye on the interests of the people re clean living on the back benches.
MADDIE	It isn't the people, it's the newspapers.
McT	That's true.
C-S	Well the newspapers are the people in a sense — they are the channel of the government's answerability to the governed. The Fourth Estate of the realm speaking for the hearts and minds of the people.
Mrs. E	And on top of that they're as smug a collection of inaccurate, hypocrytical, self-important, bullying, shoddily printed sick-bags as you'd hope to find in a month of Sundays, and dailies, and the weeklies aren't much better.
C-S	They're not all that inaccurate.
CHAMB	You can't ignore them.
MADDIE	Nothing would happen if you did. They've got more people writing about football than writing about you and that's in the cricket season — they know what they're about.

C-S	The press, you see, is not just an ordinary commercial enterprise like selling haberdashery.
MADDIE	Yes it is.
C-S	Yes I know it is, but it is also the watchdog of democracy, which haberdashery, by and large, is not.
MADDIE	If the press is all that, you should be asking <u>them</u> about chasing after anything in a skirt, which they do. You should have a Select Committee on it — "Your Committee doesn't think it right for journalists to carry on as if there was no tomorrow."
WITHEN	Thank you —
MADDIE	You're just as entitled to enjoy yourself as they are.
WITHEN	Thank you very much —
MADDIE	You should tell them to mind their own business.
WITHEN	Paragraphs 1 and 2 read and agreed to.
MADDIE	<u>I</u> would —

(*The* CHAIRMAN *looks at her.*)

Sorry. *(she starts writing)*

WITHEN	Paragraph 3.
MADDIE	*(with her hand up)* Paragraphs 1 and 2 ....
WITHEN	.... read and agreed to. Paragraph 3.
MADDIE	*(with her hand up)* .... read and ....
WITHEN	.... agreed to ....
MADDIE	.... agreed to ....
WITHEN	Paragraph 3.
MADDIE	Thank you. Sorry.

WITHEN	Paragraph 3. Your Committee and their predecessors in the last session have had before them the papers laid before the House including the written depositions (appendix A) and memoranda (appendix B).
	(ALL *turn over to next page.)*
	Paragraph 4. Your Committee also had before them a large assortment of press cuttings on this and related matters (appendix C). Your Committee did not feel that any purpose would be served by calling all the authors of these articles, which were in any case frequently anonymous or pseudonymous, and invariably uncorroborated.
Mrs. E	Amendment, Mr. Chairman.
WITHEN	Yes, Mrs. Ebury.
Mrs. E	Paragraph 4, line 4. After "invariably uncorroborated" insert "and actuated by malice".
WITHEN	Amendment proposed. After "invariably uncorroborated" insert "and actuated by malice". In favour?
ALL	*(except* C-S) Aye.
WITHEN	Against.
C-S	No.
WITHEN	Amendment stands. *(to* MADDIE) Alright?
MADDIE	Act....
McT	...u...a...*(pause)*...ted
CHAMB	by ...
MADDIE	by ...
C-S	Malice
MADDIE	Mal...
Mrs. E	iss ... (MADDIE *looks up)* ...<u>ice</u>.

WITHEN	Mrs. Ebury in brackets.
MADDIE	*(pause)* In brack—ets.
WITHEN	No, no just put her in brackets. *(apologetically)* It's her first time you know.
ALL	Oh yes .... naturally ....time to settle down ....
WITHEN	Soon get the hang of it. Paragraph now ends "invariably uncorroborated and actuated by malice".
CHAMB	Amendment, Mr. Chairman.
WITHEN	Yes, Mr. Chamberlain.
CHAMB	Insert after "malice" the words "and a cynical pursuit of cheap sensationalism".
WITHEN	Amendment put. In favour?
ALL	*(except* C-S) Aye.
WITHEN	Against.
C-S	No.
WITHEN	Amendment stands.
CHAMB	*(to* MADDIE) Me in brackets.
MADDIE	...cyn...
CHAMB	*(at* MADDIE's *speed)*.... ical pursuit
MADDIE	....ical purs....
CHAMB	....uit of....
MADDIE	....suit of....
CHAMB	....cheap sens....
MADDIE	....cheap sense....

36

CHAMB   ....ationalism.

MADDIE   ....ationalism.

            (This may have been fractionally faster than the last amendment.)

WITHEN   That's right.   You see, you're improving all the time.

ALL   Oh yes .... getting the hang of it ......

McT   Amendment, Mr. Chairman.

            (McTEAZLE scribbles on a piece of paper.)

WITHEN   Yes, Mr. McTeazle.

McT   After "sensationalism" insert "through a degrading obsession with dirty linen among the Pecksniffs of Fleet Street."

            (He hands paper to MADDIE)

WITHEN   I don't think these unnatural practices are very ....

McT   He's a character in Dombey and Son —

WITHEN   *(lying)*   I am well aware he's a character in Dombey and Son.

C-S   Chuzzlewit.

WITHEN   *(with spirit)*   Chuzzlewit yourself, Cockie.   Amendment put. Favour?

ALL   *(except C-S)*   Aye.

WITHEN   Against.

C-S   No.

WITHEN   Amendment stands.   Paragraph now reads —

C-S   Amendment, Mr. Chairman.

WITHEN   Yes, Mr. Cocklebury-Smythe.

C-S   Before the words "and a cynical pursuit etcetera" insert the words "in some cases, possibly".

WITHEN	Amendment put. All in favour?
C-S	Aye.
WITHEN	Against.
ALL	*(except* C-S) No.
WITHEN	Amendment fails. *(to* MADDIE) Paragraph now reads ....
MADDIE	*(reading from the draft)* "Paragraph 4. Your Committee also had before them a large assortment of press cuttings on this and related matters (appendix C). Your Committee did not feel that any purpose would be served by calling all the authors of these articles, which were in any case frequently anonymous or psuedonymous, and invariably uncorroborated *(reads from her notebook)* and actuated by malice and a cynical pursuit of cheap sensationalism *(reads from paper passed to her by* McTEAZLE) through a degrading obsession with dirty linen among the Pecksniffs of Fleet Street. I'm sitting on your slip. *(to* McTEAZLE) Sorry.
McT	*(looking at the others)* A slip — just a slip.
WITHEN	The question is put that that last paragraph stand as part of the report.
C-S	Division, Mr. Chairman.
WITHEN	Division, Committee divided. Mr. Chamberlain.
CHAMB	Aye.

(MADDIE's *hand has gone up.*)

WITHEN	*(to* MADDIE) The Com-mit-tee div-id-ed.
MADDIE	.... divided. Then what do I do?
WITHEN	Then you draw a line down the middle.

(The CHAIRMAN *goes to the blackboard and draws a line down the middle and generally demonstrates on the blackboard.)*

WITHEN	You write 'ayes' up there on the left and 'noes' up there on the other side and when I call out their names you write them down on one side or the other, according to what they say.
	Mr. Chamberlain.
CHAMB	Aye.
WITHEN	Mrs. Ebury.
Mrs. E	Aye.
WITHEN	Mr. McTeazle.
McT	Aye.
WITHEN	Mr. Cocklebury-Smythe — National Union of Journalists.
C-S	No — I have to make a living in my spare time too, you know.
WITHEN	Three — one
MADDIE	Just like the football results.
WITHEN	*(warmly)* Just like the football results. *(to Members)* Isn't it?
ALL	Oh yes .... so it is .... what a good thought ....
WITHEN	Paragraph 4, read and agreed to. Mr. Cocklebury-Smythe, M.P., N.U.J.; dissenting.
	Paragraph 5.
MADDIE	You don't need all these paragraphs, you know ....
WITHEN	"Your Committee ...."
MADDIE	You're just playing into their hands. (WITHEN *glares at her.*) It's just my opinion.
WITHEN	Paragraph 5. "Your Committee ...."

McT   *(to* MADDIE)   Whose hands?

WITHEN   *(to* McTEAZLE)   For God's sake —

MADDIE   The press.   The more you accuse them of malice and
            inaccuracy, the more you're admitting that they've got a
            right to poke their noses into your private life.   All this
            fuss!   This whole report can go straight in the waste paper
            basket.   All you need is one paragraph saying that M.P.s
            have got as much right to enjoy themselves in their own
            way as anyone else, and Fleet Street can take a running
            jump.

WITHEN   Miss Gotobed, you may not be aware that the clerk tradi-
            tionally refrains from drafting the report of a Select
            Committee.

MADDIE   And anyway, there's no malice in it.   You've got that wrong,
            too.

WITHEN   Paragraph 5!

C-S   She's quite right, of course.   It is simplistic to speak of
            malice.

WITHEN   Smart alec-paragraphs about innocent tripe-and-onions with
            tittian voluptuaries? — if that's not malice I don't know
            what is.

MADDIE   They only write it up because of each other writing it up.
            Then they try to write it up <u>more</u> than each other — it's
            like a competition, you see.

C-S   *(puzzled)*   A free press is competitive naturally ....

MADDIE   No, the <u>writers</u>.   They're not writing it for the people, they're
            writing it for the writers writing it on the other papers.   "Look
            what I've got that you haven't got."   There don't have to be
            any <u>people</u> reading it at all so long as there's a few journalists
            around to say, "Old Bill got a good one there!"   That's what
            they're doing it for.   I thought you'd have worked that out
            by now.

C-S   *(taken aback)*   Not really.

40

MADDIE   You see, you don't know the first thing about journalism.

> (ALL *laugh at* COCKLEBURY-SMYTHE.
> MADDIE *stands up — unfolds one of the news-*
> *papers on her desk and holds it in front of her,*
> *between her and the Committee so that it*
> *obscures her skirtless, slipless state of undress from*
> *the Committee but not from the audience. She*
> *walks to the front of the committee table. The*
> *Committee react to the photograph on the paper*
> *facing them.)*

The <u>pictures</u> are for the people.

ALL   Strewth!

> *(The door opens to admit Mr. French, who enters*
> *and hangs up his coat. As the Committee look at*
> *him, MADDIE turns and returns to her desk,*
> *folding the newspaper.)*

CHAMB   Hello, French.

FRENCH   *(to* CHAIRMAN, *without seeing* MADDIE)   Mea maxima culpa.

C-S   Merde.

WITHEN   All present and correct.   *(to* MADDIE)   Amend list of members present.

C-S   *(to* MADDIE)   French ....

MADDIE   *(to* FRENCH)   Enchanté ....

C-S   No .... no .... Mr. French, Miss Gotobed.

FRENCH   How do you do, so sorry to interrupt.   *(looking at the blackboard)*   What's that?

> (FRENCH *sits down. He has a white silk handker-*
> *chief showing in his breast pocket and he uses this*
> *to wipe his brow. He does this once or twice*
> *during the scene.)*

WITHEN   A blackboard.   No .... No .... I was just ...

> *(He looks round for something to wipe the board*

*but there's nothing to hand so he takes the under-
pants out of the brief case and uses them.)*

.... our clerk, Miss Gotobed, has been assigned to this
Committee on the recommendation of I think you-know-
who —

FRENCH   Who?

MADDIE   Fanshawe.

WITHEN   — need I say more?   Her experience of committee work is
somewhat limited and I was just explaining one or two of
the finer points.

FRENCH   Of course.

WITHEN   Well, as I was saying on that last Division Cocklebury-
Smythe is under the 'noes'.

McT   Pecksniff.   Chuzzlewit.

C-S   Yes —

McT   Sorry.

C-S   Not at all.

(The CHAIRMAN *has hurriedly wiped the board
clean and is putting his underpants back into his
brief case.)*

FRENCH   What is that?

WITHEN   Pair of briefs.

FRENCH   What are they doing in there?

WITHEN   It's a brief case.   Paragraph 5.

FRENCH   What stage are we at Mr. Chairman.

WITHEN   Second reading of the draft report, Mr. French.

FRENCH   When was the first reading?

WITHEN   Haven't you gone through it?

FRENCH   Yes.   Last night.

WITHEN   That's when it was.   Do you really want me to go through
          the whole thing again?   It's pure formality.

FRENCH   That may be so, but there is a way of doing things, and if
          we're not going to do them in that way then let it be shown
          in the proceedings of this Select Committee that the Committee
          voted on that point.

WITHEN   Very well.

                    (very rapidly)

C-S   Propose.

McT   Second.

WITHEN   Favour.

ALL   *(except* FRENCH)   Aye.

WITHEN   Against.

FRENCH   No.

WITHEN   Carried.

                    *(Even more rapidly, absolute breakneck speed
                    because it's pure ritual.)*

FRENCH   Division.

WITHEN   Division.   Mr. Chamberlain.

CHAMB   Aye.

WITHEN   Mr. Cocklebury-Smythe.

C-S   Aye.

WITHEN   Mrs. Ebury.

Mrs. E   Aye.

WITHEN   Mr. French.

FRENCH   No.

WITHEN   Mr. McTeazle.

McT   Aye.

WITHEN   Carried.

MADDIE   Line down the middle?

WITHEN   Line down the middle.

            (FRENCH *is slightly surprised by this.*)

WITHEN   Committee divided 4 — 1.

MADDIE   Home win.

WITHEN   Home win.   Mr. French lone scorer for visitors.

FRENCH   I beg your pardon?

WITHEN   The terminology of committee practice is in a constant
            state of organic change, Mr. French.   If you can't keep up
            you'll be no use to us.   Paragraph 5.

FRENCH   Excuse me, Mr. Chairman.

WITHEN   Yes, Mr. French?

FRENCH   We haven't heard any evidence.

WITHEN   Evidence about what Mr. French?

FRENCH   You know very well, evidence about what — evidence
            about 128 Members of Parliament making fools of them-
            selves over a latter day du Barry and bringing the House
            into public ridicule and disrepute.

WITHEN   *(heatedly)*   Do you believe everything you read in the papers,
            Mr. French?

FRENCH   *(also heatedly)*   I wish to have this exchange of views recorded
            in the minutes.

44

WITHEN	*(at* MADDIE's *speed, to* FRENCH) Do you believe every-thing you read in the papers, Mr. French?
C-S	*(at* MADDIE's *speed, to* FRENCH) It is true that some of us have been feeling up ....
	(Pause. ALL *react to* "feeling up" *with some trepidation.* COCKLEBURY-SMYTHE *continues innocently.)*
	.... to now that evidence as such does not exist in these matters.
ALL	Hear, *(pause)* hear!
	(FRENCH *has taken some time to cotton on to the reason for the rate of speech, because the other Members have tactfully ignored* MADDIE. FRENCH *goes through various stages of bewilderment and suspicion before noticing* MADDIE's *writing speed.)*
FRENCH	Just a minute — excuse me — is Miss Gotobed a secretary/clerk of the Clerks Department?
WITHEN	Why d' you ask?
C-S	She can do 40 words a minute.
FRENCH	Shorthand?
C-S	No — talking.
Mrs. E	She is seconded from the Home Office.
FRENCH	What is her job there? A manicurist?
MADDIE	I'm a typist.
WITHEN	Miss Gotobed has been recommended, by different people, I understand, in a period of some difficulty.
FRENCH	I was expecting to have Mr. Barraclough, a man of irreproach-able credentials —
WITHEN	I believe he has taken an early retirement for personal reasons.
MADDIE	Barry has?

45

WITHEN   I must insist that we get on with the proper business of this Committee.

FRENCH   *(getting hysterical)* The proper business of this Committee is to examine witnesses!

WITHEN   If you will be so patient, Mr. French, you will be reminded that paragraph 5 will take full cognizance of the evidence heard by this Select Committee in its previous incarnation during last session.

FRENCH   I was not a member then.

WITHEN   None of us were members then, Mr. French. This Committee has suffered the resignation for personal reasons of the previous membership — and for medical reasons, of the previous chairman, Sir Joshua Matlock who dislocated his hip —

MADDIE   Both hips —

WITHEN   Both hips. Nevertheless that evidence, such as it was, is something which I have given due consideration in preparing my draft report. *(to* MADDIE) Now *(generally, at* MADDIE's *speed)* Paragraph 5 read as follows. *(Normal speed)*

                  (ALL *turn to proper place in draft report.)*

            Your Committee also had the advantage of having a number of distinguished journalists regaling the Committee with the moving and heroic struggle of the British press from time immemorial to become independent watchdogs of the people's right to know; with many references to flames, torches, swords, pens, grails and the general impedimenta of chivalrous quest ....

C-S   *(giggles)* Tennyson's Disease.

WITHEN   .... Unfortunately, the witnesses were considerably less help-ful on the subject of their sources for the unsubstantiated speculations which were the chief and only reason for the witnesses being called. Your Committee therefore was unable to conclude that the aforesaid speculations had any basis in fact —

McT	Amendment, Mr. Chairman.
WITHEN	Yes, Mr. McTeazle.
McT	Paragraph 5 line 1, before the word "journalists", omit the word "distinguished".
FRENCH	Then we should examine the editors.
WITHEN	Can we dispose of amendment?
FRENCH	What about the leading article in this week's New Statesman? It refers to private information.
WITHEN	*(jeers)* Private information? Gossiping over Bristol Cream in Vincent Square?
FRENCH	That is your assumption only.
WITHEN	Where else would he pick anything up — young pup — what's-his-name —
MADDIE	Tony.
FRENCH	The editors must be in possession of hard information otherwise they would not let the reporters publish the rumours.
WITHEN	Don't be a bloody fool, man.
C-S	I'm afraid that that does not always follow, Mr. French.
FRENCH	What about the Times? You're not suggesting that the Editor of the Times — a man of irreproachable credentials — *(heatedly to* MADDIE) Mr. French proposed: that the Editor of the Times ....
WITHEN	Not so quickly please.
FRENCH	*(slowly)* Mr. French proposed ....
McT	*(to* Mrs. EBURY) What do you think of it so far?
Mrs. E	Rubbish!

FRENCH   *(continues slowly)* .... that the Editor of the Times
            (resuming his normal speed) — whatever his name is —

MADDIE   Willy.

WITHEN   *(impatiently)*   This is already dealt with in appendix B.
            The Times has published no rumours, it's only reported
            facts, namely that other, less responsible papers are
            publishing certain rumours.   <u>That</u> is a written deposition
            from Editor   *(Rifling through Appendix B)*

FRENCH   It is not.   It is a memorandum from one of the Whips
            who bumped into him in the interval at Covent Garden.
            Can anyone of us truthfully say that we have <u>really</u>
            examined the Editor of the Times?

CHAMB   No.

C-S   No.

WITHEN   No.

Mrs. E   No.

McT   No.

MADDIE   Not really.

                    (or from stage right round the table.)

WITHEN   I must insist that we get back to bloody amendment.
            The question is put — to omit the word "distinguished"
            before the word "journalists".   All in favour.

ALL   *(except C-S and FRENCH)*   Aye.

WITHEN   Against.

C-S   )
            No.
FRENCH)

WITHEN   Arsenal 3 Newcastle 2.   Scorers McTeazle, Chamberlain
            and Ebury for Arsenal.   French and Cocklebury-Smythe,
            own goal, for Newcastle.

FRENCH   What the hell are you talking about?

48

WITHEN	Kindly watch your language — you're not on terraces now, y'know
Mrs. E	And there are ladies present.
FRENCH	Alright! Cards on the table! I didn't want to be the one to bring this up, but I rather expected to learn on arriving here today that one of our number — I exclude Mrs. Ebury of course — had seen fit to resign from this Committee. I refer to the paragraph in today's Mail about the tete-a-tete at the Côte d'Or.
Mrs. E	Cock
FRENCH	Coq d'Or.
Mrs. E	Double cock.
FRENCH	Without either a resignation, or alternatively our joint repudiation of the story, I don't see how this Committee can have the confidence of the House.
Mrs. E	Ballocks.
FRENCH	That is not an expression which I would have associated with you, Mrs. Ebury.
Mrs. E	I don't need you to tell me my problems.
WITHEN	*(aside to* MADDIE) The Committee deliberated.
FRENCH	I find the Committee's silence on this point significant.
WITHEN	Well, we all thought it was you.
FRENCH	I left for my constituency on Friday evening and returned this morning. The only meal I've had this weekend in a London restaurant was tea on Friday at the Golden Egg in Victoria Street.
C-S	L'Oeuf d'Or?
McT	Were you with a woman?
FRENCH	I was with the Dean of St. Paul's.

49

McT	Is she titian-haired?
CHAMB	Come off it McTeazle. *(kindly to* FRENCH*)* French, can anyone corroborate your story?
FRENCH	The Dean of St. Paul's can.
CHAMB	Apart from her.
FRENCH	We had Jumbo Chickenburgers Maryland with pickled eggs and a banana milkshake. The waitress will remember me.
CHAMB	Why?
FRENCH	I was sick on her shoes.
C-S	Your story smacks of desperation. Even so you have done us the honour of volunteering your account, so let me reciprocate. I was at various times at Crockfords, Claridges and the Golden Cock, Clock, the Old Clock in Golden Square, not the Coq d'Or.
CHAMB	I was at the Crock of Gold, Selfridges and the Green Cockatoo.
McT	I was at the Cockatoo, too, and the Charing Cross, the Open Door, the Golden Ox and the Cuckoo Clock.
WITHEN	I was at the Cross Cook, the Fighting Cocks, the Green Door, the Crooked Grin and the Golden Carriages.
	(What is happening is difficult to explain but probably quite easy to recognise: the four of them have instinctively joined in an obscuration, each for his own defence. By the time the CHAIRMAN *speaks they have all begun to send* FRENCH *up.)*
C-S	I forgot — I was at the Golden Carriages as well as Claridges, and the Odd Sock and the Cocked Hat.
WITHEN	I didn't see you at the Cocked Hat — I went on to the Cox and Box.
McT	I was at the Cox and Box, and the Cooks Door, the Old Chest, the Dorchester, the Chesty Cook and — er — Luigis.

ALL   Luigis?

McT   At Kings Cross.

CHAMB   I was at Kings Cross; in the Cross Keys and the Coal Hole,
           The Golden Goose, the Coloured Coat and the Côte
           d'Azure.

C-S   I was at the Côte d'Azure —

WITHEN   So was I.

Mrs. E   I was at the Coq d'Or.

CHAMB   (incautiously)   I was at the Coq d'Or too.
                   (Short pause but everybody comes to his rescue.)

McT   So was I.

C-S   The Coq d'Or?   Oh yes, I was at the Coq d'Or.

WITHEN   I saw you there — I was there with a voluptuous young
           woman.

C-S   Good heavens, I hope you didn't see me with mine.

CHAMB   Fantastic woman I took there — titian hair, green eyes,
           dress cut down to here.

McT   We held hands under the table — (with a crude gesture)
           voluptuous, you've no idea.

WITHEN   Don't talk to me about voluptuous — mine was tittian
           like two Boticellis fighting their way out of hammock.

                   (During the above speech FRENCH is becoming
                   increasingly agitated, and MADDIE increasingly
                   angry. She gets out her copy of the Sun and
                   opens it to the centre page spread.)

C-S   Wonderful figure of a woman —

                   (MADDIE gets up and crosses to FRENCH,
                   holding the Sun.)

FRENCH   (shouts)   One of you is telling the truth!   Where's the Mail!

51

(MADDIE *slams the Sun down on the table in front of* FRENCH, *open at the centre page spread and stands back to await his reaction.)*

WITHEN   That's the Sun.

(FRENCH *does an enormous double-take at the pin-up.)*

FRENCH   *(shrieks)*   Aagh! — it's you!

MADDIE   Yes.

(FRENCH *grabs* MADDIE *by the back of the blouse as she moves to go back to her desk; buttons pop and fly leaving* FRENCH *holding her blouse and* MADDIE *in her bra.)*

ALL   *(looking at* MADDIE)   Strewth!

(MADDIE *walks back to her seat, taps her pencil on the desk.)*

MADDIE   Paragraph 6.

FRENCH   "Maddie Takes It Down!

"Madeleine Gotobed, 21, is a model secretary in Whitehall where she says her ambition is to be Permanent Under Secretary.   Meanwhile, titian-haired, green eyed Maddie loves being taken out, but says the men tend to look down on a figure like hers — whenever they get the chance!" — disgusting — "Matching bra and suspender belt, Fenwicks £5.35.   French knickers, Janet Reger £8.95."   *(to* MADDIE) You were in the Coq d'Or!

(The Division Bell goes off.)

MADDIE   I was in the Coq d'Or, the Golden Ox, Box Hill, Claridges and Crockfords —

WITHEN   Division Bell, Mr. French.

MADDIE   — and the Charing Cross, the Dorchester, the Green Cockatoo, Selfridges and the Salt Beef Bar in Rupert Street with Deborah and Douglas and Cockie and Jock.

(MADDIE *has pointed to these four.   Pause —* WITHENSHAW *looks relieved.)*

And with Malcolm in the Metropole —

> *(The committee's next words are just rattled off underneath MADDIE's speech which continues without pause.)*

WITHEN   Move to adjourn.

C-S   Second.

WITHEN   All in favour?

ALL   *(except* FRENCH)   Aye.

WITHEN   Meeting adjourned for ten minutes.

> *(The Committee hurriedly shuffle a few pieces of paper together, leaving all the newspapers behind, and arrange themselves to make their exits in a body, ignoring MADDIE who chants on.)*

MADDIE   *(continuing until all but* FRENCH *have left)*   and in the Mandarin, the Mirabelle and the Star of Asia in the Goldhawk Road.   I was with Freddie and Reggie and Algy and Bongo and Arthur and Cyril and Tom and Ernest and Bob and the other Bob and Pongo at the Ritz and the Red Lion, the Lobster Pot and Simpsons in the Strand — I was at the Poule au Pot and the Coq au Vin and the Côte d'Azure and Foo Luk Fok and the Grosvenor House and Luigi's and Lacy's and the Light of India with Johnny and Jackie and Jerry and Joseph and Jimmy, and in the Berkeley, Biancas, Blooms and Muldoons with Micky and Michael and Mike and Michelle — I was in the Connaught with William and in the Westbury with Corkie and in the Churchill with Chalky.   I was at the Duke of York, the Duke of Clarence and the Old Duke and the King Charles and the Three Kings and the Kings Arms and the Army and Navy Salad Bar with Tony and Derek and Bertie and Plantaganet and Bingo.

> *(During the above speech the Committee all exit through the wrong door, return and re-exit.   The door closes, leaving only* FRENCH *with* MADDIE.)

(yells after them)   And I wouldn't have bothered if I'd known it was supposed to be a secret — who needs it? *(normal voice)*   I sometimes wonder if it's worthwhile trying to teach people, don't you Mr. French?

FRENCH   Miss Gotobed, this is going to teach them a lesson they'll never forget.

MADDIE   I hope so.

FRENCH   I have to go and vote. Please be here in about ten minutes. *(He approaches her with blouse still in hand.)*

MADDIE   Excuse me .... *(she takes blouse)* .... Somebody's coming.

(At this moment a loud voice is heard approaching.)

Could you show me the ladies cloakroom, please.

(She grabs the rest of her clothes and her handbag. FRENCH takes her coat from the rack and puts it over her shoulders and opens the door. MADDIE exits, FRENCH follows. As soon as the door closes, the other opens and two men enter — but they are in another play.)

NEW-FOUND-LAND

a play in one act

CHARACTERS

ARTHUR   A very junior Home Office Official

BERNARD   A very senior Home Office Official

*The House of Commons overspill meeting room in
the tower of Big Ben, set as for 'Dirty Linen'. A
lot of newspapers and reports are lying around on
the main committee table.*

*(ARTHUR appears carrying a file of papers and
shouts loudly into the door through which he
enters, as though calling to someone at a distance.)*

ARTHUR   *(shouts)* Here's an empty one!

    *(BERNARD enters immediately. ARTHUR shouts
at him at the same volume. Everything ARTHUR
says has to be shouted, throughout.)*

ARTHUR   It's the only one.   The Minister said up here — he'll find us
alright.

    (They approach the table and sit at it.)

BERN   Frightful mess.

    *(ARTHUR shuffling newspapers comes across
something.)*

ARTHUR   Strewth!

    *(An appallingly loud noise as Big Ben strikes 4
from just over their heads. ARTHUR flinches.
BERNARD looks around vaguely. The last
stroke finally dies away.)*

BERN   What was that?

ARTHUR   4 o'clock.

    *(Considerable pause. BERNARD takes out his
wallet and an envelope containing a very old
£5 note.)*

BERN   I bet you have not seen one of these for a while ....
it's a fiver I once won off Lloyd George, you know.

ARTHUR   Yes.

BERN   It's a good story ....

ARTHUR   Very, very good.

BERN   I was a green young man at the time, and he was ....

whatdoyoucallit ....

ARTHUR   Prime Minister.

BERN   Prime Minister.   Even so, I knew him quite well, or rather
          my father did.

ARTHUR   Your father knew Lloyd George, yes.

BERN   He'd come to our house in Queen Anne Place.   You could
          hear Big Ben from there.   That's what reminded me.

ARTHUR   Yes.
          This is the file on that applicant for British citizenship.
          What do you think?

          (ARTHUR *moves to sit next to* BERNARD *so
          that he can speak loudly into his ear.* ARTHUR
          has a bulky file, including a photograph, to show
          BERNARD.)

BERN   What?

ARTHUR   These naturalization papers.   We're supposed to be
          advising the Minister.

          (BERNARD *examines the document at consider-
          able length.*)

ARTHUR   I'd like to have your opinion.

          (Finally BERNARD *raps the document
          authoritatively.)*

BERN   This is an application for British naturalisation.

ARTHUR   Yes.   Does he look alright to you?

BERN   He's got a beard.   The Minister won't like that.

ARTHUR   *(nods)* No, then.

          (Considerable pause.)

BERN   He asked me for my views about French, you know.

ARTHUR   French?

58

BERN   Poor French. Out of touch. Do you know what he said
            to me about French?

ARTHUR   Who — the Minister?

BERN   Know what he said?

ARTHUR   What?

BERN   *(shouts)* Do you know what he said about French?
            (normal voice) Called him a booby.

ARTHUR   *(Gives up.)* Really.

                    (Considerable pause.)

BERN   I was in Belgium, having a look round the village church of
            Etienne St. Juste, when I had the good fortune to receive a
            slight injury. The morning after my return to London, I
            remember, was one of those rare February days when winter
            seems to make an envious and premature clutch at the spring
            to come. I breakfasted by the window. The panes of glass
            in the window suddenly pulsed *(makes the sound)* — woomph
            -woomph — as though alive to the shock-waves of distant
            guns. I started to sob. But it was only a motor coming up
            the road. It stopped. The doorbell jangled below stairs,
            and there was a knock at the morning room. Lloyd George
            was shown in. My father had already left for the City, as
            he liked to put it. He owned an emporium of Persian and
            oriental carpets in Cheapside, which was indeed in the City,
            and that is where he had gone. So there I was, a young
            Lieutenant, barely blooded, talking to the Prime Minister
            of the day, and receiving ribald compliments on the shell
            splinter lodged in my lower abdomen. The shell itself had
            made a rather greater impact on the church of Etienne
            St. Juste. I explained my father's absence, but Lloyd
            George was in no hurry to leave. It was then that he made
            his remark about French. "What do they say in the field?"
            "Were they glad to see him go?" I replied tactfully that we
            all felt every confidence in Field-Marshal Haig. "Yes" he
            said "Haig's the man to finish this war. French was a
            booby." That is what he said. *(Pause.)* Presently, Big
            Ben was heard to strike 10 o'clock. Lloyd George at once
            asked me whether it was possible to see Big Ben from the
            upstairs window. I said that it was not. "Surely you're
            wrong", he said, "are you absolutely certain?" "Absolutely

                                                                    59

certain, Prime Minister." He replied that he found it difficult to believe and would like to see for himself. I assured him that there was no need. The fact was, my mother was upstairs in bed making out her dinner table: she had the understandable, though to me unwelcome, desire to show me off during my leave. Lloyd George pressed the point, and finally said "I will bet you £5 that I can see Big Ben from Marjorie's window." "Very well" I said, and we went upstairs. I explained to my mother that the Prime Minister and I had a bet on. She received us gaily, just as though she were in her drawing room, Lloyd George went to the window and pointed "Bernard" he said "I see from Big Ben that it is 4 minutes past the hour. The £5 which you have lost" he continued "I will spend on vast quantities of flowers for your mother by way of excusing this intrusion. It is small price to pay" he said "for the lesson that you must never pit any of the five Anglo-Saxon senses against the Celtic sixth sense." "Prime Minister" I said "I'm afraid Welsh intuition is no match for English cunning. Big Ben is the name of the bell not the clock." He paid up at once ....

.... and that was a fiver which I can tell you I have never spent.

(He shows the note to Arthur.)

How they laughed. "Marjorie" he said "that boy of yours does not miss a trick." I left then, to take a cab to Dr. Slocombe in Pall. Mall. When I returned I saw Lloyd George for the last time. He was coming down the steps. Nervousness caused me to commit the social solecism of trying to return his money. "Keep it" he said "I never spent a better £5." He got into the back of the motor and waved cheerily and called "You will go far in the Army." Well, he was wrong about that. And he was not entirely right about Haig either. It was the Americans who saved <u>him</u>.

ARTHUR   This applicant is American.

(Pause.)

BERN   An <u>American</u> with a beard? Oh dear .... of course, in those days it was the other way round. It was difficult to get British nationality <u>without</u> a beard. A well bearded and moustachioed man stood an excellent chance with the Home Secretary. A man with a moustache but no beard was often given the benefit of the doubt. A man with a beard and <u>no</u> moustache, on the other hand,was considered unreliable and probably fraudulent, and usually had to remain American for the rest of his life. Does he have property?

(From here on ARTHUR *refers to the file.)*

ARTHUR   He is associated with a stable in Kentish Town.

BERN   Epsom Downs?

ARTHUR   No — Kentish Town.

BERN   A racing stable?

ARTHUR   It seems to be more of a farm really ....

(Considerable pause.)

BERN   Did you say he farms in Kentish Town?

ARTHUR   Yes.

BERN   Arable or pasture?

ARTHUR   It does seem odd doesn't it?

BERN   I imagine that good farming land would be at a premium in North London.   Is he prosperous?

ARTHUR   He has an income of £10.50 per week.

BERN   Hardly a pillar of the community, even with free milk and eggs.

ARTHUR   No.

BERN   He is either a very poor farmer indeed, or a farmer of genius — depending on which part of Kentish Town he farms.

ARTHUR   He's not exactly a farmer I don't think .... he has other interests.   Publishing.   And he runs some sort of bus service.

BERN   Publishing and buses? And a farm. Bit of gadfly is he?

ARTHUR   Yes. And community work.

BERN   They all say that.

ARTHUR   Yes.

BERN   Anything else?

ARTHUR   There's a theatrical side to him.

BERN   Do you mean he waves his arms around?

ARTHUR   No — no — he writes plays, and puts them on and so on.
           He seems to have some kind of theatre.

BERN   Oh dear, yes. A theatrical farmer with buses on the side,
           doing publishing and community work in a beard .... are
           we supposed to tell the Minister that he's just the sort of
           chap this country needs? Does he say why he wants to be
           British?

ARTHUR   Yes, because he's American.

BERN   Well he's got a point there.
           Do you know America at all?

ARTHUR   Do I know America!

BERN   Americans are a very modern people, of course. They are a
           very open people too. They wear their hearts on their
           sleeves. They don't stand on ceremony. They take people
           as they are. They make no distinction about a man's back-
           ground, his parentage, his education. They say what they
           mean and there is a vivid muscularity about the way they
           say it. They admire everything about them without reserve
           or pretence of scholarship. They are always the first to put
           their hands in their pockets. They press you to visit them
           in their own home the moment they meet you, and are
           irrepressibly goodhumoured, ambitious, and brimming with
           self-confidence in any company. Apart from all that I've
           got nothing against them.

ARTHUR   My America! — my new-found-land!
62

(ARTHUR takes surprising flight.)

Picture the scene as our great ship, with the blue riband of
the Greyhound of the Deep fluttering from her mizzen,
rounds the tolling bell of the Jersey buoy and with fifty
thousand tons of steel plate smashes through the waters
of Long Island Sound. Ahead of us is the golden span of
the Brooklyn Bay Bridge, and on the starboard quarter the
Statue of Liberty herself. Was it just poetic fancy which
made us seem to see a glow shining from that torch held
a thousand feet above our heads? — and to hear the words
of the monumental goddess come softly across the water:
"Give me your tired, your poor, your huddled masses, the
wretched refuse of your teeming shore ...."? The lower
decks are crowded with immigrants from every ghetto in
the Continent of Europe, a multitude of tongues silenced
now in the common language of joyful tears.

(By now BERNARD has fallen asleep.)

The men wave their straw hats. Shawled women hold up
their babies, the newest Americans of all, destined, some
of them, to become the captains and the kings of indus-
trial empires, to invent the modern age in ramshackled
workshops, to put a chicken into every pot, an automobile
by every stoop, to organize crime as never before, and to
fill the sky over Hollywood with a thousand stars! Nor
is the promenade deck indifferent to the sight. Many a
good hand is abandoned on the bridge tables, many a
diamante purse forgotten on the zebra-skin divans, as
glasses are raised at the salon windows. New York!
New York! it's a wonderful town! Already we can see
the granite cliffs and towers of Manhatten, and Staten
Island too, ablaze like jewels as a million windows give
back the setting sun, and soon we have set foot on the
New World.

The waterfront is seething with life. Here and there
milling gangs of longshoremen scramble on the ground
for the traditional dockets to work the piers, and
occasionally two of them would give savage battle with
their loading hooks. At the intersection of Wall Street
with the Bowery the famous panhandlers, the wretched
refuse of cheap bar-rooms, huddle in doorways wrapped
in copies of the Journal. Behind us a body plummets to
the ground — a famous millionaire, we later discover, now

lying broken and hideously smashed among the minis-
cule fragments of his gold watch and the settling flurry
of paper bonds bearing the promises of the Yonkers
Silver Mining and Friendly Society.   The air is alive with
bells and sirens.

But now a new sound! — ghostly trumpets and trombones
caught in the swirling eddies of the concrete canyons!
— and a few more steps bring us to Broadway.   Every
way we turn excited crowds are thronging the electric
marquees.   Sailors on shore-leave are doing buck-and-wing
dances in and out of the traffic, at times upon the very
roofs of the yellow taxis bringing John Q. Public and his
girl to see the sights of Baghdad-on-the-Subway.   In threes
and fours, sometimes in lines a hundred wide, the midship-
men strut and swing up the Great White Way chorusing
the latest melodies to the friendly New Yorkers, to the
dour Irish policeman swinging his night-stick on the corner,
to the haughty hand-on-hip ladies of the night who have
seen it all before.   But it's time to tip our hats and turn
aside, for the tall columned shadow of Grand Central
Station falls across our path.   We are booked on the
Silver Chief.

Begging the pardon of a cheerful Redcap we are directed
with a flashing smile to the Chattanooga train.   Night is
falling as we cross the Hudson.   Friendships are struck,
hipflasks are passed around, and cigar-smoke collects
around the poker schools.   A cheerful Redcap with a
flashing smile fetches ice.   The Silver Chief surges through
the night.   When we retire behind the curtain of our comfortable berths the roaring blackness outside the windows
is complete, save for the occasional pillar of fire belching
from the mines and mills of Pennsylvania.

And it is to fire that we awake; woods blazing in tangerine
shades of burnt umber and old gold — the Fall has come
to New England.   The train drives relentlessly on, dividing
whiteframe villages from their churches, and children from
their hoops.   And the woods give way to suburbs, and the
suburbs to stockyards and slaughterhouses and the wind is
slamming off the Great Lake as we pull round the Loop into
Chicago — Chicago! — it's a wonderful town!   Tight-lipped
men in tight-buttoned overcoats and grey fedoras join the
poker games.   C-notes and G-notes raise the stakes.   Shirt-

sleeved newspapermen of the old school throw in their cards in disgust and spit tobacco juice upon the well-shined shoes of anyone reading a New York paper. A cheerful shoeshine boy with a flashing smile catches nickels and dimes as he crouches about his business. The air is scented with coffee and ham and eggs.

And the countryside is changing too as we swing south. Blue skies and grass are as one on the azure horizon of Kentucky. Soon thoroughbred stallions race the train on either side. Young girls in gingham dresses wave from whitewood fences. But again untamed nature overcomes the pastures — we climb through mountain ash and hickory into the Tennessee Hills. Tumbledown wooden shacks, rusty jalopies give no hint of life but the eye learns to pick out hillbilly groups sullenly looking up from their liquor jugs and washboards.

We doze and wake in thundery oppressive heat. Thick groves of oak and magnolia darken the windows of the speeding train — and encroach, too, upon the fly-blown shutters of white-porticoed mansions which stand decaying sill-high in jungle grasses that once were lawns. Atlanta is burning! A phlegmatic Redcap serves fried chicken and bottles of cherry soda. The poker players have departed. Big bellied, red-eyed men in white crumpled suits swig from medicine bottles of two-year-old sour mash bourbon. Enormous women in taffeta dresses stir the air with pan-handled fans advertising Dr. Pepper Cordials. The train bursts Alabama-bound into the blinding flatlands where cotton is king and a man and a mule dominate a thousand acres of unfenced fields like a heroic sculpture. The sun hangs over them like a threat. Our wheels break into clattering echo as the iron girders of the Mississippi Bridge slash across the windows, sending shock-waves to make the glass pulse woomph-woomph around us. Far below, a boy on a raft looks up wistfully at the mournful howl of the Silver Chief, but that old green river rolls them along toward the bend where chanting Negroes heave on the rudder-poles of barges bringing pig-iron from Memphis and hogs-heads from St. Louis — and where the last of the river boats working out of Natchez rides the oily waters like a painted castle way down yonder to New Orleans.

The train slows down, crawling through the French quarter

of the City on the Delta.   The sun hangs like a copper pan over boarding houses with elaborately scrolled gingerbread eaves.   In the red-lit shadow of wrought-iron balconies octaroon Loreleis sing their siren songs to shore-leave sailors, and sharp-suited pimps push open saloon doors, spilling light and ragtime to underscore the street cries of old men selling shrimp gumbo down on the levee.   A dignified Red-cap hums an eight-bar blues — how long, how long, has that evening train been gone? — at the back of the car a one-armed white man takes a battered cornet from inside his shirt and picks up the tune with pure and plangent notes. Soon the whole car — bible salesmen, buck privates from Fort Dixie, majorettes from L.S.U., farm boys and a couple of nuns — is singing the blues in the night *(He lights a cigarette — American brand).*   The sun drops into the smoke stacks of Galveston like a dirty dinner plate behind a sofa. The train picks up speed.   When we retire behind the cur-tains of our comfortable berths the roaring blackness out-side the windows is complete save for the occasional pillar of fire flaring up from oil wells under the cooling scrub.

BERN   *(waking up)*   Ever seen one of these before, Arthur? — I won this fiver off —

ARTHUR   *(violently)*   Ten thousand head of cattle on the hoof, packed together in a rolling river of hide and horn, meet our eye when we are woken with steak and eggs by a surly Redcap! The Silver Chief is on the Chisholm trail to Abilene! Amarillo — Laramie — El Paso — Dodge!   The wheels roll, the rails curve, past the crude wooden crosses of Boot Hill where lean-jawed men who once rode tall now lie in gun-slingers' graves.   And beyond, the open prairie. Tumbleweed races the train on either side.   Lone riders whoop and wave their hats from lathering ponies and are lost to sight as we hit the dustbowls of Oklahoma!   Where once the corn stood high as an elevator boy, and the barns shook with dancing farmhands changing partners to a fiddler's call, now screen doors bang endlessly in the wind which long ago covered up the tyre tracks of bone-rattling pick-ups taking the Okies on their tragic exodus to the promised lands of El Dorado.   How easy now on the gleam-ing rails, now carving a path through the heart of the grain lands where the gigantic mantis-forms of harvesters trawl the golden ocean that fills the breadbaskets of America!

66

We climb with the sun out of the plains .... Carson City
— Sioux City — Wichita — Tucson — Tulsa — Albuquerque
— Acheson, Topeka and the Santa Fe. Snow capped
mountains shimmer on the horizon, and still we climb.
From the observation platform at the rear we watch stone-
faced Indians, watching the shadows turn the thousand-
foot walls of the Colorado River deep red and purple.
Huddled in our blanket we sleep. Once we seem to wake
to a nightmare of acrylic lights — against a magenta sky
huge electric horseshoes, dice, roulette wheels and giant
Amazons with tasselled breasts change colour atop marble
citadels that would beggar Kubla Khan. But when the
caucasian Redcap shakes us all is peace. The Silver
Chief is rolling through vineyards and orchards, a sun
bathed Canaan decked with peach and apricot, apples,
plums, citrus fruit and pomegrantes, which grow to the
very walls of pink and yellow bungalows to the very edge
of swimming pools where near-naked goddesses with honey-
brown skins rub oil into their long downy limbs. Could
this be paradise? — Or is it after all, purgatory? — for
look! — there, where picture palaces rise from the plain,
searchlights and letters of fire light up the sky, and a
screaming hydra-headed mob surges, fighting and weeping,
around an unseen idol — golden calf or cadillac, we do not
not stop to see — for now beyond the city, beyond America,
beyond all, nothing lies before us but an endless expanse
of blue, flecked with cheerful whitecaps. With wondering
eyes we stare at the Pacific, and all of us look at each other
with a wild surmise — silent —

> *(The door opens. Several men and a woman barge
> in as though they owned the place, chatting among
> themselves.)*

ARTHUR You've got the wrong room, buster!

DIRTY LINEN

conclusion

The room is occupied by two men, both Home Office Civil Servants, both formally dressed (ARTHUR and BERNARD)

ARTHUR has a file of papers among other paraphernalia.

(The door opens and in come WITHENSHAW, COCKLEBURY-SMYTHE, McTEAZLE, Mrs. EBURY, and CHAMBERLAIN chatting. WITHENSHAW goes to confront ARTHUR at the secretary/clerk's desk.)

WITHEN   What?

ARTHUR   I'm sorry — this is a Home Office Departmental Meeting.

WITHEN   What are you doing here?

ARTHUR   We are meeting here for the convenience of the Home Secretary who has to answer the Division Bell.

WITHEN   Well, I'm very sorry, but as you can see this room is occupied by a Select Committee.

ARTHUR   On the contrary, as you can see, it is occupied by a Home Office Departmental Meeting.

WITHEN   Yes, but we were here first.

McT   Hello, Bernard — still soldiering on?

BERN   *(standing up)* Mr. McTeazle, isn't it? — yes — yes — I was just showing young Arthur here — I bet you haven't seen one of these for a while. *(produces £5 note)*

        (Meanwhile WITHENSHAW is writing another note for MADDIE. By this time COCKLEBURY-SMYTHE, McTEAZLE, CHAMBERLAIN and Mrs. EBURY have sat down. The HOME SECRETARY enters with a rush of words and sits in the CHAIRMAN's place.)

HOME   Good afternoon, gentlemen — what a large gathering — difficult case? — I thought it was only that American — goodness me, let's keep things tidy can we?

(He starts stacking the mess of newspapers on the table.)

An orderly table makes for an orderly meeting.

(He has the Mirror in his hands.)

Strewth!

tit—tit—tut—tut—oh! *(Sees WITHENSHAW whilst folding the pin-up picture away.)* Hello Malcolm.

ARTHUR   This lady and these gentlemen are here for another meeting, Minister.

WITHEN   Sorry, Reg, first come first served.

HOME   Are you Send—In—A—Gumboot?

WITHEN   What?

HOME   Are you Rubber Goods Import Quota?

WITHEN   No — no — we're Moral Standards in Public Life.

HOME   Oh yes, so you are — no hard information, I hear.

WITHEN   We're not sure, Reg — something came up this afternoon.

HOME   Yes, well, I'm sorry to pull rank on you, Malcolm ....

> *(The Select Committee Members stand up; ARTHUR and BERNARD sit down.)*

.... but I've got to deal with a very sensitive and difficult case —

> *(The HOME SECRETARY looks at WITHENSHAW's note to MADDIE, who by this point has entered and is hanging up her coat.)*

What's this? "Forget the Golden Cock ....

> (WITHENSHAW *snatches it out of his hand and tears it into four and scatters the pieces.)*

MADDIE   *(to HOME SECRETARY)*   Hello, what are you doing here?

HOME   How do you do? My name's Jones. *(to WITHENSHAW)*

As I was saying you must have the room of course.

> (ARTHUR and BERNARD *stand up,*
> WITHENSHAW *crosses to his Chairman's seat*
> *and the Select Committee sit down again. The*
> HOME SECRETARY *continues, the underlined*
> *words aside to* MADDIE.)

Noblesse oblige — say no more — anyway I'm expected at an Intrusion of Privacy Sub-Committee of the <u>Forget Le Coq au Vin, Le Poule au Pot</u> Departmental Committee on Rag and Bone Men, Debt Collectors and Journalists.

ARTHUR   But Minister what about ....?

> (ARTHUR *holds out the folder. The* HOME
> SECRETARY *whips out a pen and signs with a*
> *flourish.)*

HOME   One more American can't make any difference.

> (BERNARD *approaches* WITHENSHAW *with the*
> *£5 note.)*

BERN   Mr. Withenshaw, isn't it? Take a look at this — there's quite a story behind it —

> (WITHENSHAW *snatches the note and tears it*
> *into four pieces.* BERNARD *is crestfallen.)*

WITHEN   *(shouts)* Get out!

HOME   A word in your ear, Malcolm. Have you got time for a drink?

> *(The Home Office men leave.)*

WITHEN   Oh, I'd love ....

> (FRENCH *enters and crosses to his place.)*

.... not really Reg.

HOME   I'll give you a ring.

> *(The* HOME SECRETARY *leaves. An uncomfortable*
> *silence descends as the Select Committee settle down.)*

WITHEN   Well now .... where were we .... *(pause.)*

FRENCH   Mr. Chairman ....

WITHEN   Oh yes .... you were about to make a point, Mr. French.

FRENCH   Thank you, Mr. Chairman.   I have been giving this matter
         a great deal of thought during our short adjournment.
         I think I can say that never has the phrase O tempora O
         mores come so readily to the lips.

C-S   Meaning what?

FRENCH   Meaning, "Oh the times Oh the — "

C-S   I know what it means.   Why was it on your lips?

FRENCH   I am not a whited sepulchre, Mr. Chairman.   I take no
         pleasure in crying "j'accuse".   But I have been talking
         to Miss Gotobed.   She has poured out her heart to me
         and I may say it was a mauvais quart d'heure for the
         Mother of Parliaments. Not since Dunkirk have so many
         people been in the same boat — proportionately speaking
         of course.   I am faced now with a responsibility which I
         would dearly like to be without, but it seems I am presented
         with, to put it in plain English, a fait accompli.   I have
         struggled with my conscience seeking an honourable
         course and not wishing to drag this noble institution
         through the mud.

WITHEN   A very responsible attitude, Mr. French.

McT   )
CHAMB) Hear, hear!

FRENCH   Thank you.   I think I have indeed found a way.   I pro-
         pose we scrap the Chairman's Report as it stands and
         replace it with a new report of my own drafting.

         (He holds up a piece of paper.)

         (He clears his throat and starts to read.)   Paragraph 1.
         In performing the duty entrusted to them your Commi-
         ttee took as their guiding principle that it is the just and
         proper expectation of every Member of Parliament, no
         less than for every citizen of this country, that what they
         choose to do in their own time, and with whom, is ....

MADDIE   *(prompting)* .... between them and their conscience.

FRENCH   *(simultaneously with* MADDIE*)* .... conscience, provided
         they do not transgress the rights of others or the law of

                                                                    73

the land; and that this principle is not to be sacrificed to that Fleet Street stalking-horse masquerading as a sacred cow labelled "The People's Right to Know".

Your Committee found no evidence or even suggestion of laws broken or harm done, and thereby concludes that its business is hereby completed.

WITHEN   Is that it?

FRENCH   It's the best I can do.

WITHEN   How am I going to spin that out until Queen's Jubilee?

FRENCH   You can't.   This is the last meeting of this Committee, unless you want to do it your way.

WITHEN   No — no —

       (MADDIE *throws her report and all her appendices in the waste paper basket.*)

C-S   You'll have to get your peerage another way.

WITHEN   The P.M. will kick my arse from here to Blackpool.

C-S   Services to sport.

McT   I would like to applaud Mr. French's understanding attitude and his stroke of diplomacy.

CHAMB   Hear, hear.

Mrs. E   I move that Mr. French's report is put to the Committee.

C-S   Second.

WITHEN   Have you got that, Mis Gotobed?

MADDIE   Yes, Malcolm.

WITHEN   All in favour.

ALL   Aye.

WITHEN   Against.

74

(silence)

FRENCH   Arsenal 6 — Newcastle nil.

WITHEN   Thank you, Mr. French.

FRENCH   Not at all, Mr. Chairman.

> *(French takes his breast pocket handkerchief out, which is now the pair of knickers put on by* MADDIE *at the beginning, and wipes his brow.)*

FRENCH   Toujours l'amour.

> *(Big Ben chimes the quarter hour.)*

MADDIE   Finita La Commédia.

**** END ****

TOM STOPPARD previously wrote 'After Magritte' and 'Dogg's Our Pet' for Inter-Action. His other plays include 'Enter a Free Man', 'The Real Inspector Hound', and Evening Standard Award winners 'Jumpers', 'Rosencrantz and Guildenstern are Dead' and 'Travesties'. The latter two also won Tony Awards on Broadway. He has also written for radio and television, and one novel, 'Lord Malquist and Mr. Moon'. He began his writing career in journalism, joining the Western Daily Press, Bristol in 1954 as a junior reporter. Subsequently he worked for the Bristol Evening World and after 1960 he was a freelance journalist in Bristol and London. He lives in Buckinghamshire with his wife and four children.

ED BERMAN, an expatriate American, founded Inter-Action Trust in 1968. He now works as the Artistic Director of Inter-Action Productions (including The Ambiance Lunch-Hour Theatre Club, The Almost Free Theatre, the Fun Art Bus and the Dogg's Troupe). As ED.B., he has written six plays produced in London including 'Sagittarius', 'Virgo' and 'The Nudist Campers Grow and Grow'.

For the Ambiance, he has directed several plays, among them the premieres of John Arden's 'Squire Jonathan', 'The Window' by Frank Marcus, James Saunders' 'Dog Accident' and 'Savoury Meringue', and Tom Stoppard's 'Dogg's Our Pet'. Like other members of Inter-Action's co-operative, he divides his time between the production company and work in schools, youth clubs, mental hospitals, community centres, playgrounds, remand homes and the streets.

Most of his time is now spent as Programme Director of Inter-Action Trust, creating new community arts and action projects such as "City Farms 1 : The Fun Art Farm" and youth employment programmes. He still manages to direct some ten plays a year, mainly for children's and community theatre, and to perform in two hundred-odd shows. Prof. R. L. Dogg (a pseudonym) writes verses for children.

In real life he is the head of the Father Xmas Trade Union, Chairman of the Save Piccadilly Campaign, Hon. Treasurer of the Fair Play for Children Campaign and Chairman of the National Association of Arts Centres.

A Harvard graduate and former Rhodes Scholar, he now lives in the Inter-Action co-operative in Kentish Town, London. He became a naturalised British Citizen on April 5th 1976, the day of the first public showing of 'Dirty Linen' and 'New-Found-Land'. This was celebrated by a party at the House of Commons (because the banqueting rooms at the House of Lords were booked solid).

INTER-ACTION is a charitable trust founded in 1968 by Ed Berman to stimulate community involvement in the arts, especially through the use of drama and creative play, and to experiment in theatre/media and their social applications.

The work of Inter-Action is broadly divided into two categories — theatre and community work. In addition to the Ambiance/Almost Free activities (described on the back cover of this volume), Inter-Action Productions embraces the work of the Dogg's Troupe, Infilms and the Fun Art Bus. All activities are administered by a co-operative of artists and community workers whose time is shared between the production company and out-going work in the community.

The community work side of the trust has fifty members who live and work in Kentish Town, London Borough of Camden, where Inter-Action is in the process of completing construction of the first purpose-built community arts centre in the U.K. This centre will house the rehearsal and administrative functions of Inter-Action Productions. More importantly, the new centre will provide a base for the community related activities of the organisation.

Among these activities are numbered the following:

> The Advisory Service, which gives free advice to community, arts and other voluntary groups, in the fields of finance, organisation and programming. The Advisory Service has recently pioneered "New Job Horizons" — a programme to provide bursaries for unemployed school-leavers to work and be trained with community-based voluntary organisations. This project has been jointly funded by private industry and governmental support. The Service has a branch called NUBS — Neighbourhood Use of Buildings and Space. NUBS is concerned with community participation in low-cost rehabilitation of existing space and facilities for local recreational and social use.

> Inprint — the publishing unit of Inter-Action. Publications include Advisory Service Community Action Handbooks and Playscripts from seasons at the theatre club.

> Inter-Action Game Method and Training, which is the approach to group work developed by Inter-Action. Sessions based on this method are used in hospitals, schools, youth clubs and a wide variety of special problem groups. Training courses in Group work, Video, Playleadership, Community Arts and Theatre and Community Action are available for Youth and Community Workers, Teachers, Activists, Social Workers, Dramatists, Artists, Parents, Volunteers and Therapists.

78

In addition, Inter-Action has set up the first City Farm in Great Britain — The Fun Art Farm located in Kentish Town. This was created by rebuilding derelict buildings with voluntary help. It has a barnyard, stables, indoor riding school, allotments, community gardens and a large workshop. These facilities provide the setting for many community arts and theatre projects.

Other aspects of Inter-Action's community work include the Community Media Van, a studio-on-wheels for community action, a community play programme and a project for school refusers sponsored by the Inner London Education Authority.

The skills, training and prestige of the Theatre side of the work are applied to an innovatory approach in the use of communications for community work. In 1970, a Council of Europe report described Inter-Action as "the most exciting community arts project in Europe .... Inter-Action is praised by almost everyone — from both inside and outside the establishment."

Tom Stoppard

Rosencrantz and Guildenstern are Dead
Jumpers
The Real Inspector Hound
Enter a Free Man
Albert's Bridge
After Magritte
Artist Descending a Staircase
and Where Are They Now?
Travesties

a novel
Lord Malquist and Mr Moon

from
Faber & Faber